MEOW

Our Alphabet

Our alphabet
is a puzzle—
full of mystery
full of glory.
We rearrange
its pieces
to teach
or tell a story.
The words
are always
different
but the letters
are the same.
Mix
endless worlds
from 26.
Writing
is a game.

Beep Beep

VROOMM

Write!

POEMS BY AMY LUDWIG VANDERWATER

ILLUSTRATED BY RYAN O'ROURKE

WORDSONG

AN IMPRINT OF BOYDS MILLS & KANE

New York

For Elizabeth Harding, with gratitude
—ALV

To DMH, for all your birthday cards
and letters that never cease to
bring a smile to my face —RO

Text copyright © 2020 by Amy Ludwig VanDerwater
Illustrations copyright © 2020 by Ryan O'Rourke

For information about permission to reproduce selections from this book,
please contact permissions@bmkbooks.com.

WordSong
An Imprint of Boyds Mills & Kane
wordsongpoetry.com
Printed in China

ISBN: 978-1-68437-362-8
Library of Congress Control Number: 2019904391

First edition
10 9 8 7 6 5 4 3 2 1

Design by Barbara Grzeslo
The text is set in Neutraface.
The illustrations were created with oil paint and colored in Photoshop.

CONTENTS

Timeline

I was a new writer
just learning how
I scribbled
I drew
I listened.

Then wow!

I sang all the letters.
I matched them by sound.
I used finger spaces.
I moved words around.

Best of all
let me tell you
a secret I found—

Writing a sentence
is building a tower
block after block
hour by hour.

I am a writer.
And writing is power.

WRITING
A SENTENCE
IS BUILDING
A TOWER
BLOCK AFTER BLOCK
HOUR BY
HOUR
I AM A
WRITER
AND WRITING IS POWER

How to Begin

First: Find a place.
It doesn't matter where.
Perhaps beside your heater
or cozy in a chair.
(You do not need a whole room.
Writers often share.)

Next: Bring some things—
a rock that makes you smile
your favorite stuffed rhinoceros.
Place these in a pile.
(Treasures keep you company.
You may be here a while.)

Last: Look around
with open heart and eyes.
Let your writing brain be brave.
You may be surprised.
(Writing is discovery.
Not knowing can be wise.)

Same Feeling

Did you ever open up your fridge
hungry for a snack
staring
seeking something good—
but nothing good stares back?

Did you ever look at all your clothes
uncertain what to wear
searching
for a favorite shirt—
one that is not there?

If you did, you recognize
how writer's block can paralyze.
But unlike a snack or shirt
one idea multiplies.

Ideas spread like wildflowers
when you move your hand.

Ideas (like Peaches)

Ideas (like peaches) grow on trees
but choosing is not always quick.
So place a ladder in your head.
Settle in before you pick.

Stretch your arms.
Feel drops of rain.
Hold a basket to your chest.
Ask yourself, *Which one is ripe?*
Which idea will taste best?

Fresh thoughts sprout in every brain
and each sweet crop is new.
Your life is full of fruits
that must be picked by you.

Is your paper blank?
Do ideas feel out of reach?
Grab your ladder.
Climb your mind.
Pick one like a peach.

If I Were an Octopus

I'd grab eight pencils.
All identical.
I'd fill eight notebooks.
One per tentacle.

Thank You Notes

It is easy to feel thankful.
I barely have to try
to fill these little cards with
what I'm thankful for and why . . .

Dear Monarch Butterfly,
Thank you for flying
by our front stoop this morning.
You fluttered joy into my heart
when I was feeling sad.

Dear Crazy Socks,
Thank you for not caring
if you match or not.
You hug my feet.
You make my mouth smile.

Dear Man at the Corner Market,
Thank you for setting out
bundles of roses—
I smell every color
on my way to school.

Love,
Me

Writing about Reading

I am usually
cheerfully lost in my reading.

An author
drops me in a character's shoes
gives me a mystery
dips me in history
wraps me in science
or poems or news.

I am lost without breadcrumbs.

But
sometimes I'm not.
I pause and admire.
I reread and jot.
I scribble my feelings.
I copy a line.

My notes are my breadcrumbs.

Each one is a sign
guiding me back
to words on the shelf
leading me deep
into books and myself.

Anything Can Grow

When I plant a writing seed
    anything can grow.

Even in the summer
    I can make it snow.

I invent a person
    who never lived before.

I compose a peaceful song
    when news is shouting *war*.

I tell a tale of unicorns
    lively under pines.

In life I do not have a boat.
    I sail one on these lines.

I can turn day into night.
I can do this when I write
with my hand in black on white.

Anything can grow.

Wyoming

Two weeks ago
I knew nothing of Wyoming.

Now horses gallop between my ears.
Geysers surge in my veins.
Sacajawea leads Lewis and Clark
through the prairie of my brain.

I wander old ghost towns
strain to hear forgotten songs
watch rodeos behind my eyelids.
Elk kick dry dirt in my face.

I take a break
        from my state report
                to get a drink of water.

One day
I will ride a wild horse
will hike in Sacajawea's hidden footprints
will pull a Grand Teton pebble
from my sneaker.

One day
I will live
in this perfect rectangle of Wyoming
that two weeks ago
I could not locate on a map.

Patience

Here, poem! Here, poem! I wiggle my fingers.
Gently, I whisper. My shy poem lingers.
It hesitates, tilting its head to one side.
It's trying to trust me with eyes open wide.

Here, poem! Here, poem! I do want to hold it
to snuggle its words. And then I will fold it
into my notebook. I try to be still.
My poem will come to me. I know it will.

Here, poem! Here, poem! I wait for so long
singing a soft, smitten, poemlove song.
I sit like a pretzel to offer my lap.
My poem seems sleepy. Perhaps it will nap.

Oh, poem! Oh, poem! At last you are here.
You breathe with a rhythm I drink with my ear.
I listen as you snore a story in rhyme.
A poem needs patience. I must give you time.

My Story

I close my eyes so I can find
A memory I wish to keep.
Maybe I will write about
When my new kitten fell asleep
Right on my chest. I smelled her breath.
I felt her twitch in dreams of play.
That's it! I'm ready to begin.
I know what I will write today.
Now I note what I remember
Going slowly, part-by-part
Making pictures, writing words.
You can read what's in my heart.
Sofía—sunny, fluffy kitty
Tail to nose, all orange fur
On my chest and fast asleep.
Read: You'll fall in love with her.
(You might even start to purr.)

Opinion

I wrote my essay about phones
how people do not look at faces.
They gaze at screens and hurry places
but I think we should see each other.

I gave good reasons (it got longer).
Examples made my essay stronger—
I go biking with my brother.
Mom and I read books together.
I included quotes from friends.
One said, *Texting never ends.*

My hope is that when someone reads
my paper, he or she concedes—
We all would feel much less alone
if we looked up, put down the phone.

Revision Is . . .

a little bit bummer
a little bit *Yes!*
a little bit risk
a little bit guess
a little bit play
a little bit fear
a little bit fuzzy
a little bit clear
a little bit imagine
a little bit do
a little bit old
a little bit new
a little bit shuffle
a little bit loss
a little bit add
a little bit toss
a little bit maddening
a little bit fun
a little bit faith
and then . . .
    you're done.

Conversation

I tear out your pages.
I write on your face
My cursive is crooked
I am a disgrace.
You deserve better.
Why do you stay?
Notebook, if you could
would you run away?

You are my person.
Will I leave you? Never.
Your cursive is charming.
Your entries are clever.
I love wearing secrets
and art on my face.
Keep writing, my child.
I am your safe place.

24

My Little Sister Writes

When my little sister writes
a little book for me
I can tell
she drew her pictures
very carefully.

I ask if she will read it
and she says
she plans to be
an author
and I tell her
that I have to disagree.

She is an author now.
An author who is three.

Writing Is for Everyone

Writing is for everyone.
I know this to be true
for you cannot be me
and I cannot be you.

You do not think
the things I think.
I do not choose
the words you choose.
We laugh at different jokes.
We hold opposing views.

One of us writes articles.
One of us writes plays.
Writing is a fingerprint.
It helps us touch our days.

A variety of voices
creates the sweetest chorus.
Our words on paper say
We're here.
We write.
You can't ignore us.

Final Edit

I revised.
Now I must edit.
I always do.
I should not dread it.

I read out loud to help me hear
what sounds imperfect to my ear—
an extra word
a misused phrase
one sentence that feels like a maze.

I read again. What do I see?
Superfluous apostrophe?

I check once more to guarantee
all is flawless as can be.
Careless errors will discredit
my hard work.
That's why I edit.

But I don't like it.
There. I said it.

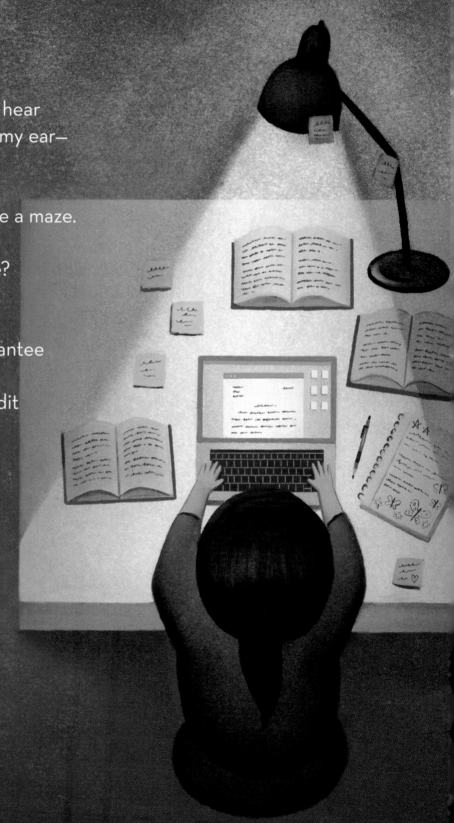

Now

I like to staple
staple a book

a book I made
made on my own

my own ideas
ideas I dreamed

I dreamed and wrote
wrote on pages

pages are portals
portals to enter

to enter
with wonder
with courage
with love.

The Pen

In a town, there is a house.
And in the house, there is a room.

And in the room, there is a boy.
And in his hand, he holds a pen.

And in the pen, swirl drops of ink.
They lead the boy to write and think.

And when he reads, the boy can see
the pen has set his stories free.

It could be you.
It could be me.

(Pens are magical, you see.)

Truth

If this oak tree had a door
it would be red
with an acorn window
and a brass door knocker
shaped like a squirrel.

If a river had a door
it would be turquoise
with a rounded top
and silver hinges
etched with small fish.

If our moon had a door
it would be sage green
with a star window
and an old opal knob
that glowed in twilight.

Everything has a door.
We write our way in.
We do.
Each word is a key.
It is.